फोंडनेस फॉर डाईती

दी फायरबॉक्स

Copyright © The Fireboxx
All Rights Reserved.

ISBN 978-1-63781-086-6

This book has been published with all efforts taken to make the material error-free after the consent of the author. However, the author and the publisher do not assume and hereby disclaim any liability to any party for any loss, damage, or disruption caused by errors or omissions, whether such errors or omissions result from negligence, accident, or any other cause.

While every effort has been made to avoid any mistake or omission, this publication is being sold on the condition and understanding that neither the author nor the publishers or printers would be liable in any manner to any person by reason of any mistake or omission in this publication or for any action taken or omitted to be taken or advice rendered or accepted on the basis of this work. For any defect in printing or binding the publishers will be liable only to replace the defective copy by another copy of this work then available.

यह थीसिस मेरे सह-लेखक, आकाश की मदद और समर्थन के बिना संभव नहीं होती। मैं इस अवसर को उन सभी लोगों के प्रति अपनी कृतज्ञता का विस्तार करने के लिए भी लेना चाहूंगा जिन्होंने पुस्तक के माध्यम से मेरा साथ दिया।

मैं अपने सीईओ सर अकाश को धन्यवाद देना चाहूंगा, जिसने मुझे इस विषय पर प्रोजेक्ट करने का मौका दिया यह पुस्तक सभी को पॉजिटिव वाइब्स दे बस यही हमारा मैन मोटिव है

मैं पुस्तक के सह-लेखक, आपके मित्रों, आपके फायरबॉक्स के परिवार को धन्यवाद देना चाहूंगी, हम सभी फायरबॉक्स के परिवार के सदस्य हैं।

अंत में, मैं अपने परिवार और दोस्तों को अपनी शोध अवधि के दौरान उनके प्रोत्साहन के लिए धन्यवाद देना चाहूंगा।

क्रम-सूची

पावती (स्वीकृति)	vii
1. Compiler	1
2. Akash Gupta	2
3. Annesha Sen	4
4. Debanjana Ghatak	7
5. Taniya Soul	14
6. Raghav Raja	18
7. Ritwika Ghosh	20
8. Mala Garg	22
9. Annu Yadav	25
10. Manisha Goyal	28
11. Dr. Rani Bansal	31
12. Geetanshu Jindal	33
13. Kavita Sai Matai	36
14. Bineesh Balakrishnan	40
15. Dinakar Reddy	43
16. Pawan Dubey	45
17. "भक्ति की नींद"	47
18. "मुझमें साई..तुझमें साई.."	48

पावती (स्वीकृति)

यह फॉण्डनेस ऑफ डाईयति एंथोलॉजी सबके अंदर छुपी हुई उस पॉजिटिव वाइब्स की आवाजों का उत्सव है 'fondness of diety का अर्थ है देवता का शौक। लिखते समय शब्दों का काम है, इसमे छपी हुई सारी कविताएं हर इंसान से जुड़ी हुई है जो उनके मन की बात तथा उनका भगवान को लेकर भगति भाव दिखता है ।

इतने सारे लेखन समूहों की तरह कविता, कहानी, शायरी कलेक्टिव अन्य लेखकों से संपर्क की आवश्यकता से पैदा हुआ था। हम एक ऐसा वातावरण बनाना चाहते थे जिसमें कविता बाहर निकले, निर्जन और बिना सेंसर (कम से कम दूसरों द्वारा अगर पूरी तरह से स्वयं द्वारा नहीं), जहां इसे गंभीरता से लिया जाएगा।

रेट्रोस्पेक्ट में, हमारे प्रयासों को पारंपरिक, चुनौतीपूर्ण श्रेणियों में कला (और विशेष रूप से लेखन) में चुनौती देने वाले बढ़ते आंदोलन के हिस्से के रूप में देखा जा सकता है।

1
COMPILER

2
Akash Gupta

Akash Gupta, an enthusiastic common man, a writer & a poet by passion But, he has a strong desire to create something extraordinary. He is in love with stories and poems. Even though he belong to a middle-class family,from Bengal, he never forgot to dream.
"You can achieve anything if you have the spirit to fight"

प्रलय

दोस तू तो दोसी मै
और, जाम तू तो मदहोशी मै,
गीता का ज्ञान मै
तेरे सारे कुकर्मो का परिणाम मै..
श्रिस्ति का निर्माता मै
तो विनाश भी तो करता मै...
हर युग मै लेता अवतार
करता तेरे जैसो हैवानो का संघार...
कंश रावण तो एक थे
मगर यहाँ हर गली मै दुर्योधन है...
पैसो के लिए अपने बाप को मरते
अपने माँ बहेनो तक ये नहीं छोड़ते...
जो पाप तू है कर रहा
उसका हिसाब मै रख रहा
जब पाप करने से नहीं डरा
तो परिणाम से क्यों डर रहा..
खोलूंगा जब मै अपनी तीसरी आँख
कर दूंगा इस सृष्टि का विनाश..
लाऊंगा मै प्रलय फिर एक बार ...

3
Annesha Sen

Annesha Sen has her own writing blog and has been associated with many campaigns and pages. She is the author of ebook "The light of a thousand lighting bugs " .She has also been published in many different anthology paperbacks

Jewels and treasures

He is explained to be the supreme power.
He is conceived as being :
omnipotent and omniscient.
He has already written down your story.
You just only need to edit and complete it.

He will plant seeds for you
you just need to water it.
Think of what you want and let it go ,
it will float back to you in its own way.
God will speak to you in a thousand ways .
You just need to learn how to communicate.

Whenever you choose to be someone
who isn't damaged .
You won't have to carry
the weight of your past.
You will stop bleeding .
And start healing from inside.
You will know ,
how to flaunt your flaws also.

Everytime when you are losing
you should know that ,
he is relocating something new
something which is meant for you.
He will help you to find your jewels.

There is beauty in everything
even in silence.
You just need to have faith.
And the rest will fall in its own way.
He will prepare you to be
his courageous soldier ,
to fight your own battles.

He will not accept any acts of vandalism.
He will trust your acts of Benevolence.
He will mend your heart.
He will help you find your twin flame.
He will make your life intoxicating ,
full of discoveries and treasures.
Just be grateful to him for every bit of it.

4
Debanjana Ghatak

Debanjana is a simple girl and down to earth by nature. She is an ardent lover of Nature, animals, Literature and a believer of God. She loves to dream and enjoy dwelling in her fairy tale land. She loves to enjoy the tiny rays of happiness hidden in the smallest moments of life. In short she describes herself as a dreamer and believer.

God Loves You Unconditionally

A beautiful hilly area from there the whole town can be viewed. It was evening already and I had to take an interview which I was planning to conduct for years. At last my friend said yes, so I was rushing to that beautiful spot but due to my clumsiness or may be out of over excitement I fell on the ground and hurt my left knee. It was bleeding badly but I always carry medicine with me so I applied on it and tied properly with my handkerchief. Bleeding stopped but pain was there so in sloth speed I reached to the point and found that my friend had already reached and playing with sheep. My friend, Jesus loves animals whether it is a dog, cat, donkey, horse or sheep. I was scared of animals but it's he who taught me to love all the animals and care for them. Now I have a dog that was rescued by Jesus from the street and he gave her to me. I named her, Laliana. I tell about Jesus to her every night and she listens to my words with full patience.

I slowly climbed up to the hilly area and it was mesmerizingly beautiful. 'You are late.' Jesus said but not in angry tone but with a sweet smile. When he smiles I forget everything. I only wish to look at him and compose poetry only on his heavenly smile. I have already written many and he loved them all. He walked towards me and asked me, 'Where were you? You kept me waiting.'

'I am sorry Jesus. I was coming fast rather very fast so I fell on the ground and hurt my knee. Don't worry, I am fine now.'

'My God, come here and sit and show me your knee, I am so sorry I didn't notice that you are in pain and you walked so far just to have words with me. Forgive me darling.'

'It's okay Jesus, I am perfectly fine. Yes, pain is there but I didn't feel weak at all while walking. Your sweet and encouraging words were hovering around me and they always provide me strength.'

'Great to hear that, please sit. I can heal you if you allow me to do so.'

I sat on a rock and remove the handkerchief and found blood was oozing out of my wound. Jesus sat down on the ground and looked at my knee. He closed his eyes then opened after few seconds and looked at the sky then touched my knee and said, 'Now, you are healed.' I saw tears in his eyes and asked, 'Jesus, why are you crying? Are you hurt too?'

'I am not hurt physically but I felt how much you suffered so tears came to my eyes.'

I smiled after hearing his words. He looked at me and then said, 'Darling, you will not understand this unless you feel the way I felt.'

'I am much better now so shall I start the interview?'

'Of course, I am ready.'

'Jesus, my first question is that why faith in people's heart is declining day by day?'

'Good question, it is declining because they do not trust their God. They follow their own rules and find happiness in doing so. They do not bother to spend time with God or ask Him to do a miracle. If something wrong happens they give up so easily but that is the moment when you have to trust your God, your Lord and ask Him to make it right.'

'I have many friends who laugh at me because I trust God and follow your words.'

'Yes, there are plenty of so but don't get angry with them or stop talking to them but be a good example in front of them. Don't ever force them to follow me or my words but be a righteous person and you will find one day your friends are not laughing at you but praying with you.'

'Now my second question is how can we overcome sadness?'

'It takes time. If we get someone trustworthy we can share our sadness with him or her and get relieved a bit.'

'Now, it's a challenge to get someone like that to whom we can share our heart with. We can't do this with our parents even.'

'I can very well understand what you and everyone go through. If you have little faith in me then share with me your heart's content and believe me I will never reveal your secret to anyone else. It will

stay with me. I promise.'
'I do but sometimes I feel I might bore you with all my troubles and worries.'
'I am your friend. I never get bored to hear from you. Your words are precious to me. I care for you so next time don't hesitate just have faith and tell me everything and trust me.'
I was going to ask my third question but Jesus interrupted and said, 'my mother baked cake for you and me so first let's have it then we will continue. How are you feeling now?' I looked at my knee and found no scratch at all. As if I never fell on the ground. 'Miracle, you healed me completely. Thank you.' Jesus smiled and gave me a big piece of cake. We ate and praised God for gifting us such beautiful evening.
'This cake is very tasty and I will visit your house one day to know the recipe from your mom.'
'You are welcome to my house but I can tell you the recipe if you want from me.'
'Can you cook, Jesus?'
'Yes, I can and bake cake too.'
'So, one day you'll cook for me.'
'Definitely, I will.'
I asked my third question and my question was, 'how to overcome fear?' Jesus listened to the question carefully and said, 'Fear is like a villain who attacks you and try to demotivate you.'
'How to defeat this villain?'
'First you have to identify him I mean the villain. Now, this villain is invisible who secretly comes to you and attacks you with lies or you can say half truth.'
'But, how shall I know when will he come and which are his words?'
'Very simple, thoughts which tell you to give up and ask you not to trust God but to have doubt in His love are from the villain. This will lead you to depression and today's youth are mostly suffering from this.'
'You are right. I too get demoralized and depressed very often. How to overcome depression, Jesus?'

'Stop listening to the villain and rebuke him. Think positive, be optimistic, read motivational books or article, watch motivational movies or speeches, share your heart with someone you trust the most, use a journal write everything on it and talk to your God. Tell Him everything and keep your faith alive. Read His words and claim those promises made by Him in the Holy book to Him. He will definitely come to you and fight for you against the villain. All you need is to trust Him.'

'Thank you Jesus. Let us go to the next question. My next question is how should we pray?'

'First of all you need to know that prayer is nothing but a conversation with God. It is exactly the way you talk to your friends, parents or your lover. God is your heavenly father and He wants to talk to you through prayers. Normally what people does they say their prayer and end up the conversation but do they wait to hear what God wants to say to them in reply to their prayers?'

'Yes, I too do the same thing. I pray, thank Him and go.'

'Conversation means exchanging words from one person to another so it is the same process during prayer. Next time when you'll pray you must wait to hear what God wants to say to you. He loves you dearly. Don't be afraid, have faith.'

'Okay, I'll remember. Jesus, how should be our posture while praying?'

'Are you giving interview that you'll be worried about your gesture and posture? You are going to have a chat with God so relax and be at ease. You can talk to Him in any position like while walking, sitting, driving, lying, dancing, and playing. Anytime, anywhere you can call Him and talk to Him. He is yours.'

'Thank you so much. I love to talk to you.' I said. Jesus smiled and kissed my forehead. It was almost dark and I could see the stars twinkling at me and the moon was shining and smiling at both of us. Jesus said by looking at the sky, 'have you noticed the sky? Isn't it beautiful and serene? I love to look at the stars and feel the cool air. It gives me so much peace and confident.' I was looking at his calm countenance and wished to sit beside him and keep looking at him for evermore. I love and respect God but there was always a question which brought doubts in my heart. That day I wished to clear my doubt so I asked, 'Jesus, do you think God loves me even after knowing that I am not perfect?' Jesus looked at me and laughed.

'Of course He does. He loves you from the core of His heart. No one is perfect but only God is perfect. His love is pure and full of compassion. He honors you, He cares for you. You are His creation.'

'I have done many wrong things and behaved rudely with many including my parents, I even had doubts in God's promises. Aren't these sins? He can't love a sinner like me.'

'No, my little friend, God's love is beyond measure. God is the creator of the universe and He loves all His creations. Yes, whatever you did is not right but this can't make God love you less because He loves you unconditionally. He never said that 'I will love my children if they follow this or that rule.' No, my love, He loves you and will love you forever. He knows everything about you. He knows about your heartbreaks and happy moments. He knows about your secret desires which you never revealed to Him in your prayers. He lives in your heart and knows everything about you. So, child, do not ever doubt His love for you and feel free to talk to Him because that is what He needs from His children badly.'

'I am feeling much better now. I always felt that God loves me less because I am a bad sample.'

'This thought is once again from the villain. So beware of him and whenever such thought will appear just rebuke and think positive. Call me; I am always there to help you.'

After clearing all my doubts I checked the time and found it was already late for me to reach home. 'I want to talk to you forever but have to go so let's fix up our next meet before I bid you goodbye.' I said to Jesus. He smiled and said, 'Child, I am always there for you. Whenever you want to talk to me just call my name I'll be right in front of you. I love you so much that I want to talk to you always.'

I hugged him and thanked for giving his precious time to me. I bid him goodbye and slowly walked towards my home. I could hear some faint voices calling out my name. Slowly those voices grew louder and clearer. I could properly hear my mom and dad calling me. I too tried to assure them that not to worry because I was almost home but they couldn't hear me. Later I found myself lying on my bed and my parents were calling me to wake up as I was already late for my office. I looked at my parents then my bed next my teddies and my dog, Laliana and then I finally realized that I was with Jesus in my dream. I felt little sad because it was just a dream but later I felt that it wasn't any ordinary dream but the most beautiful dream I have ever seen. My parents and dog left the room and I sat and thanked Jesus for coming in my dream and answering all the questions. I closed my eyes and visualized his peaceful smiling face and wished to go back to that hilly area and hear his words again

5
Taniya soul

Taniya soul 22 years old, from h.p currently living in Gujarat. She writes, the way she see things, she feels. And here she express her words, her emotions by writing.

Why she believes in god?

A girl, who live in her own imaginary world with strongly believe in god.
4years back, with her way of thinking and living with imagination, her thoughts,
living the way she want till she stepped out, from her own world to the new place for her further studies was totally opposite from her imagination.

Unaware of the future, failure, success, love, hate, positive and negative things, living in the present, by focusing on the study and enjoying herself by paintings, games. Draw the things what she imagines and having faith in god.

What she paints, she feels, she exists.
"Every imagination, she realized,
Just a peace of mind, more an illusion than the real life"
Loving nature. Early morning, wake up to hear the melody chirp of birds, feel the fresh air, play in the soil, worship god. Her strength, her friend. She thought, god is with her, she is strong enough. A type of girl, who stands in front of god, talk to them. She was confident, strong, without fear, because she hasn't seen the world yet. Didn't face the obstacles.

Enjoying her life, peacefully.
"Imagination is the place where you live the way you want, then the real".
"Dream is a powerful thing, but the reality,
What may it brings,
Dream, full of reality,
Full of lies, where may it ties"

No friends, no connection, living the way she wants till she step out from home.

As she stepped out, for her further studies in the new place was totally opposite from her imagination.

Still, hope exists.

She was not yet ready for the new exposure, as it was beginning.

She started developing fear.

As she was genuine to her work and with everyone, but others they just for the selfishness come near her. Poor girl, she gets happy every time when others want to talk to her. She doesn't care whatever reason is, but she loved.

She loved to cover her loneliness. "What she thought, what are they,

More than the real, how fake they are,

Came here to make new friends,

More than the rainbow, multiple colors they show,

Seasons change in time, they changes more than they define"

Sitting in her room, day, night spent alone. Her each day, hour, minutes was getting worse day by day. She had a faith in God, and ask him.

Why I don't have any friends?

Why no one like to talk to me?

If I have or I trust, why they betray me?

Why I'm here? What's my worth is?

Why do I even exist?

What? Is this real me, or they are?

"All alone, dropping her tear,

Along with her fear, no one was near, to hear".

This thing continued, she had faced many obstacles, fight battles within herself.

Slowly, she loses faith in god but hope never.

Every time she cried, she cried like hell. No one was there. She was alone. If god exists, he would help her out. He would never see her crying, dying. It's been more than 3years, if he exists, he would never see her in pain.

She believed, no one will help you except yourself.
How did she get back to god again?
After 3years!
Deep inside, hope was still alive.
As she loses faith, alone in the place full of crowd.

Now, she put her aside from every negativity. She learned, know about life games, people's mind and meaning of life.

3years, without saying any word, observing others, learned what is the difference between the reality and the imagination.

Before, she was alone, not by choice, now she chooses her way alone by her own choice.

"Why you are stressed, what you want,
Is it less, More than the blessed"?

As she loved to feel the nature. Whenever, she looks at those pretty sky, feel the wind, talk to the moon and shining stars, enjoy hearing birds chirping, loving trees, allow her to believe, he exists.

She feels alive.
Yeah! It sounds like a stupid.

And she felt, "creatures of God". He exists, not in the permanent place, but everywhere. Wherever we go, he is with us, In every beautiful way.

"I found myself here, a world surrounded by the full of creatures, in love with the real, than the fake, for his sake".

He wants us to see, his love in the way of creature, how beautiful and real he has created for us, that no one can replace".

"The world full of natural and unnatural beauty, be the lover of real one".

She feels alive, no one by her side, but this.

She realized, she was never alone. And she wishes one day before too late, everyone, will know the real beauty, meaning of life.

Someday, no one will be with you,
Someday, they will leave you,

6
Raghav Raja

I'm an engineer by profession and a musician and an artist by passion. Art is a very powerful tool to express yourself and it also serves as a healing agent to your mental health.

Sri Guru Nanak Dev Ji

Sketch and write-up by Raghav Raja.

Guru Nanak, the first Sikh guru and the founder of Sikhism was born in Talwandi (present day Pakistan). Nanak came from a Hindu family and was surrounded by Muslim neighbours. From an early age, he broke away from his family's traditions by refusing to participate in empty rituals. He rejected idol worship and spoke out against the caste system, teaching instead the equality of all humanity. Nanak also believed in humanity and serving the public. We are all familiar with the golden three, "kirat karo (work), naam japo (meditate) and wand chhako (serve the needy)" and thus we see Nanak as an enlightened being or a Guru. His teachings also emphasized on choosing the correct words while talking, as he felt that the tongue is like a sharp knife, which kills without dropping blood. Here's a sketch of Guru Nanak Dev Ji, which took me four long days to finish. Dhan Dhan Sri Guru Nanak Dev Ji

7
Ritwika Ghosh

Ritwika Ghosh, born on August 2, 1997, daughter of Mr. Subhash Ghosh and Mrs. Shyamali Ghosh, belongs to a Bengali family. She lives in Kolkata, West Bengal. She loves to write poetries. She is an English Hons. graduated student from Calcutta University. Writing poems on various theme is her passion.

POWER OF GODDESS

I quiver, I tremble but I am forever there
My whisper still lingers within..
My essence is there and it always will be.
The insight will give way to a radiant day.
The wall may close on you, but
There will always be a way..
You think I am gone,
You think I am lost,
But close your eyes and you'll find me here.
I am your strength,
I am your stand,
I am the sword to slay the demons of despair.
I'll always stand by you in your fights.
I am your hope
I am always within you..
I am your power
I am The Goddess.

8
Mala garg

मेरा नाम माला गर्ग है मैं मोगा पंजाब से हूँ. खाना बनाना और साँई बाबा से जुड़े रहना मेरे दो शौक़ है । बाबा की असीम कृपा बनी रहे यही मेरी ज़िंदगी का सपना है

जय साईं राम ,
श्रद्धा सबूरी

श्री सच्चिदानंद सदगुरु साईनाथ महाराज की जय । भक्तों पर दया करने वाले बिगड़े काम बनाने वाले दीन दुखियों पर अपनी कृपा करने वाले साईनाथ महाराज की जय हो । जिस प्रकार वे दयानिधि करुणानिधान हैं उसी प्रकार उन्होंने मुझपर भी अपनी कृपा की वर्षा की मैं अपनी आप बीती सबके साथ साँझा कर रही हूँ । मैं साई महाराज के सानिध्य में लगभग २० वर्षों से हूँ । पहले पहल तो किसी व्यवसाय के सिलसिले में पूना गये थे वहाँ से हमारा कार्यक्रम शिर्डी का बन गया , उस समय तक मुझे बाबा के बारे में कोई जानकारी ना थी फिर बाबा का सचरित्र पढ़ा , बाबा की कथाओं में आनंद आने लगा , मेरा मन था की दुबारा शिर्डी जाया जाए उन दिनो मेरे पति बहुत बीमार थे , किसके साथ जाया जाए कुछ समझ नहीं आ रहा था , अचानक मेरी डॉक्टर मित्र का फ़ोन आया की हम सब लोग शिर्डी जा रहे हैं उसने बोला की मेरे सपनेमें आया है की तू भी हमारे साथ जा रही है मुझे और क्या चाहिए था , सारे इंतज़ाम कर शिर्डी के लिए रवाना हो गये । इस प्रकार बाबा ने मेरी मन की बात जानकर मेरी मनोकामना पूरी की । बाबा से प्रेम और श्रद्धा का बंधन और घनिष्ठ हो गया । लगभग ३ साल पहले २०१८ में बाबा के निर्वाण का १०० वाँ साल था मन फिर चाहने लगा की शिर्डी जाया जाए उसी बीच मेरी बेटी आयी फिर हम लोग बाबा के दर्शनरथ शिर्डी गये । जिस बात के लिए जिस चमत्कार के लिए मैं यह लेख लिख रही हूँ यह घटना २० जुलाई २०२० की है । मेरे बेटे को जो की स्पेशल चाइल्ड है बहुत तेज बुखार आया १५ दिन तक उसका बुखार नहीं गया सब टेस्ट करवाए बेटा तो आँख भी नहीं खोल रहा था , सब टेस्ट ठीक आए फिर अंत में उसका कोरोना टेस्ट करवाया गया जो की पॉज़िटिव आया । उसके बाद उसकी हालत और भी ख़राब होती चली गयी । किसी हॉस्पिटल में बेड अवेलबल नहीं था चंडीगढ़ लुधियाना अमृतसर हर जगह पता करवाया मुझे उसके साथ रहना अलाउड नहीं था क्योंकि मैं नेगेटिव थी अकेला उसे कहीं छोड़ नहीं सकती थी फिर बाबा से प्रार्थना की , बाबा अब आपकी कृपा के बिना अब कुछ होने वाला नहीं , अब तो आप ही हैं साई नाथ , चमत्कार करिये । कल वीरवार (गुरुवार) है मेरे साईनाथ का दिन है , जब मैं सोकर उठूँ तो मेरा बेटा बिल्कुल ठीक हो । साँई सचरित्र में मैंने आपके इतने चमत्कार पढ़े हैं बाबा कृपा करो बुधवार शाम को मैंने बेटे के माथे को छुआ तो माथा ठंडा था । मैंने सोचा दवा का टेम्परेरी असर

है घंटे बाद फिर चेक किया , शरीर बिल्कुल ठंडा था , मैं हैरान थी क्योंकि डॉक्टर के हिसाब से इसे anticorona drug के इंजेक्शन लगने चाहिए थे । इंजेक्शन भी १० दिन लगने थे उसके बाद ठीक होने के chances बनते थे , बाबा की कृपा हुई , १५-२० दिन से कुछ खा भी नहीं रहा था , थोड़ा बहुत मुँह में डाल देते थे , सुबह गुरुवार था मेरे बाबा का वार था थोड़ा खाना पीना भी शुरू कर लिया , अब से सेहत में सुधार होना शुरू हो गया . बाबा की उदी मैं लगातार इसके माथे पर लगा रही थी थोड़ी जल में घोल कर पिला भी रही थी । अब मेरा बेटा बिल्कुल स्वस्थ हो गया । बाबा का प्रत्यक्ष चमत्कार हो गया मैं बाबा की बहुत आभारी हूँ , जिस प्रकार मुझ गरीब पर कृपा की इसी प्रकार बाबा सबके सिर पर हाथ रखना ।

जय साँई राम

9
Annu Yadav

मैं चंडीगढ़ में रहती हूँ | साईं बाबा को १० साल से मानती आई हूँ | साईं बाबा की कृपा से मेरी अच्छी नौकरी लगी है | मेरा एक बेटा है जिसका नाम संश्रय है और दूसरी क्लास में पढता है | आज पहली बार बाबा के आशिर्वाद से मैंने कुछ लिखा है जिसकी प्रेरणा मुझे मेरी मित्र साक्षी ने दी है|

"ॐ साईं राम"
"जब नाम पुकारूँ"

हर काम संभव हो जाता ,
जो चाहा, जो माँगा वो सब है पाया |
जब नाम पुकारूँ साईं का ||

बिन मांगे भी सुनते साईं ,
जब नाम पुकारूँ साईं का ||

बच्चे, बूढ़े और जवान, सबकी इच्छा पूरी करते ,
जब नाम पुकारूँ साईं का ||
    ना शंका, ना घबराहट रहती कोई ,
जब नाम पुकारूँ साईं का ||

अँधेरे में इक ज्योत है साईं ,
हर पल नाम पुकारूँ साईं का ||

श्रद्धा और सबूरी का पाठ पढ़ाते साईं ,
बस मन में जाप करो तुम साईं का ||

मन कभी ना भटके पथ से ,
यूं ध्यान धरो तुम साईं का ||

शिरडी जैसा धाम ना कोई ,

साईं बिना पहचान ना कोई ||

ना धन, ना दौलत, ना माया मांगू,
बस साथ पाऊं मैं साईं का ||

तन मन धन सब अर्पण तुझको,
बस पाठ करू अब साईं का ||

हर काम संभव हो जाता,
जब नाम पुकारूँ साईं का ||

10
Manisha Goyal

मेरा नाम मनीषा है मेरी उम्र पचास साल है मुझे कविता लिखने का शौक है मै रेकी की सेकेण्ड डिग्री होल्डर हू व नेचरोपैथी मे डॉ हूं

बाबा। के चमत्कार के अनुभव

? ओम साईं राम?

बाबा के लिए मेरे अनुभव बहुत ही चमत्कारी व सुखद रहे हैं वे मेरे लिए सब कुछ हैं मां ,बाप, भाई, बहन ,एक अच्छे दोस्त ,एक सबसे प्यारे मेरे गुरु बाबा जो हर पल मुझे सही राह दिखाते हैं मैंने अपने जीवन में बहुत से चमत्कार देखे हैं वह कुछ चमत्कार मैं आप सब को बताना चाहती हूं मैं रोज मेरे साईं सीरियल देखती हूं मैंने उसमें देखा जो बाबा को बुलाता है बाबा उसके घर जरूर जाते हैं गुरुवार के दिन मैंने भी बाबा की पूजा की और बाबा से अरदास की बाबा आप सबके घर जाते हो आज मेरी इच्छा है आप किसी भी रूप में मेरे घर भी आओ और मैं आपको पहचान जाऊं और मैं घर के कामों में व्यस्त हो गईशाम को 4:00 बजे मेरे दरवाजे पर दस्तक हुई मेरे सामने पड़ोसन खड़ी थी जो साईं बाबा की किताब लेकर आई थी उन्होंने उस दिन उद्यापन किया था मुझे बड़ी खुशी हुई बाबा के भक्त से मिलकर मैं भूल गई थी कि मैंने बाबा से सुबह क्या मांगा था रात को मुझे बाबा ने याद दिलाया कि तूने मुझे बुलाया था और मैं आ गया तब मेरी आंखों में खुशी के आंसू बह रहे थे! ऐसे ही एक बार मेरी इच्छा हुई कि मैं आज बाबा को खिचड़ी का भोग लगाऊंगी मैंने खिचड़ी बनाई और मंदिर के बाहर से ही बाबा को खिचड़ी अर्पण की उस वक्त मुझे ऐसा लगा कि मेरे सामने कोई खड़ा है और जब मै ने आंखें खोली तब वहां कोई नहीं था पर मेरे बाबा ने खिचड़ी का भोग लगाया! अभी 2 महीने पहले मैंने फिशर का ऑपरेशन कराया था तब मेरी बाई जी ने चार-पांच दिन पहले काम छोड़ दिया मैं दूसरी बाई ढूंढने लगी पर जिस दिन मुझे ऑपरेशन कराना था उसी दिन मेरी पुरानी बाई जी का फोन आया और वह रो कर के नहीं लगी भाभी जी मैं आपका काम कभी नहीं छोड़ूंगी मैंने जब से आपका काम छोड़ा बीमार हो गई हूंऔर आज सुबह मुझे साईं बाबा ने दर्शन देकर कहा मेरी बच्ची परेशान हो रही है उसकी तबीयत ठीक नहीं है तुमने उसका काम क्यों छोड़ा और वह उसी दिन से काम करने आ गई अब वह भी बाबा को खूब मानती है! ऐसे ही एक बार में बहुत परेशान थी और बाजार से आते वक्त मुझे बहुत रोना आ रहा था तब मैंने बाबा से प्रार्थना की

बाबा मुझे आप दर्शन दो ताकि मेरे मन को तसल्ली मिल सके तभी एक दुकान पर साईं बाबा का बहुत बड़ा पोस्टर लगा हुआ था और अचानक मेरी नजर उस पोस्टर पर गई साईं बाबा के दर्शन पाकर मेरे मन को शांति मिली मुझ पर बाबा की बहुत कृपा है मैं कहीं भी जाती हूं किसी भी दुकान या किसी के घर भी यदि वहां साईं बाबा की फोटो या मूर्ति होती है तो वह मुझे चुंबक की तरह खींच लेते हैं और मेरा ध्यान उस तरफ चला जाता है! ऐसे ही करोना के समय मेरे गले में इंफेक्शन हो गया था कोई भी डॉक्टर मुझे बिना देखे ही दवाई दे रहा था मुझे बहुत घबराहट हो रही थी साईं बाबा की कृपा से एक डॉक्टर ने मुझे बहुत अच्छे से देखा भी और उसने कहा एंडोस्कोपी करवा लो मुझे बहुत डर लग रहा था उस समय पूरे समय में साईं साईं का जाप करती रही और मुझे पता भी नहीं चला कब मेरे गले की एंडोस्कोपी हो गई और कोई बीमारी भी नहीं निकली बहुत कुछ है लिखने को पर इतना ही कहूंगी "बाबा मुझे अपने चरणों की धूल बना ले तू तो फकीर है तेरा क्या जायेगा और तेरे चरणों में आकर यह बंदा अमीर हो जाएगा" ? ओम साईं राम?

11
Dr. Rani Bansal

My name is Dr. Rani Bansal. I am a gynaecologist in Moga Punjab.

ओम् साँई राम

साँई बाबा की जय हो । साँई के चमत्कार गिनना सबकी पहुँच से बाहर है मैं साँई का एक चमत्कार आपसे साँझा करना चाहती हूँ । मैं हर वीरवार साँई मंदिर जाती हूँ और साँई व्रत भी रखती हूँ । एक बार मैं USA गयी हुई थी तब मेरा वीरवार का व्रत आया तो मैंने बेटे को कहा की जब तुम वापिस आओगे तो मुझे साँई मंदिर जाना है जब मेरा बेटा वापिस आया तो थोड़ा लेट हो गया वो कहने लगा की आज तो thunderstorm की prediction है पर हम चलते हैं , जब हम मंदिर पहुँचे तो मंदिर बंद हो चुका था । पंडितजी बाहर खड़े थे वो कहने लगे आप कैसे खड़े हैं बेटा बोला ममी ने साँई बाबा के दर्शन करने हैं , पंडितजी उस समय ट्रैक सूट में थे , वो बोले मैं अंदर जाऊँगा नहीं (क्योंकि ट्रैक सूट में पंडितजी को मंदिर में प्रवेश वर्जित है) आप चाबियाँ ले को और माथा टेक लो और वहाँ केले का प्रसाद पड़ा है वो लेकर दरवाज़ा बंद करके चाबियाँ मुझे दे दो । मैंने पूछा पंडित जी इस टाइम आप कैसे आए थे , पंडितजी बोले मैं गैरेज को लॉक करने आया था । ये वाक्या कहता है कि यदि आप सच्चे मन से कुछ सोचते हैं तो साँई बाबा आपकी मनोकामना ज़रूर पूरी करते हैं

"। ओम् साँई राम"

12

Geetanshu Jindal

I am Sai Baba lover. Writing is my passion which gives me peace. I love to live simple life with no Regrets. Also i hate being judged or judging someone.

फोंडनेस फॉर डाईती

MY SAI BABA

I was of 18 years when, I got attached to SAI BABA. That was my first year of college and in August 2011 I went to Shirdi with my family. I was happy as for me it was more like a holiday and I was excited for everything but not for going to temple, as at that time I didn't knew much about Sai Baba. I enjoyed my journey in train and we all reached Shirdi in the evening around 6.30 p.m. The moment I stepped on the land of Shirdi I got some different kind of vibes, it was like suddenly my attitude for everything was so positive and I was feeling very happy. While we were going to hotel I was looking around and I was loving each and everything about Shirdi. When we reached hotel everyone was tired and so was i, as our journey was very long, but the hotel manager told us about "KAKAD ARATI" which was performed in the morning at 5.15 a.m and he said that it is must watch if you come to Shirdi. At that moment only I decided that I will be going to that arati and told this to my mother but she denied me as we all were so tired. That was the first magic which Baba showed me. In moments only I was feeling very fresh and energetic as if Baba himself wanted me to come to arati and he was inviting me to come there and the I somehow convinced my mother. I took a shower and reached temple at 4.30 a.m, but when I reached there, I saw a long line and people were sitting on ground and some were even sleeping. So I asked someone that why all these people are sleeping here like this, then I came to know that those people were sitting here in line from 11 p.m only so that they can attend arati standing inside temple as it opens, as only few people can enter the temple because of less space inside. Then I understood, if I have to attend arati I have to come early and sit in line. That day I didn't get to enter the temple, but next day I came early and that day I attended "KAKAD ARATI" standing inside the temple. Since then only I got attached to Baba from heart and soul, and he is everything to me now. Many a times Sai Baba keep on showing his presence to me in form of blessings and magics.

13
Kavita Sai Matai

My name is Kavita Matai. I'm working as a teacher in Kairalee Nilayam Central School Bangalore. My qualification is MSc (Chem) BEd. I have two sons. My husband is working for HAL Bangalore

ओम साईं राम
ओम श्री साईं नाथाय नमः

यह मेरे साईं का ही कर्म और आदेश है जो मैं इस पावन पुस्तक के लिए अपना योगदान दे रही हूं वरना मैं इस योग्य कदापि नहीं थी। इस अनुभव को साझा करने के लिए आज्ञा और आशीर्वाद दीजिए साईं बाबा!! बाबा के पवित्र चरणों में कोटि-कोटि प्रणाम

भक्त जब सच्चे मन से बाबा से कुछ मांगता है तो बाबा उसे जरूर पूरा करते हैं मेरा अनुभव इस कथन की पुष्टि करता है

साईं बाबा सबके प्यारे साईं बाबा- *सगुण रूप में तो वे शिर्डी में आए थे लेकिन निर्गुण रूप में भी बाबा हर जगह विद्यमान है यह मेरा अटूट विश्वास है। यह साईं सच्चरित्र से पूर्ण रूप से ज्ञात भी होता है कि बाबा विभिन्न जगहों पर संत पीर फकीर मौलाना साहब के रूप में मौजूद है ।इसी से जुड़ा है मेरा एक प्यारा सा अनुभव:*

बात 2012 की है वैसे तो मैं बाबा से 2008 से जुड़ी हूं। मेरे दोनों बच्चे अपनी स्कूली शिक्षा खत्म करने को थे तो मेरे मन में यह विचार उठने लगे कि अब मुझे नौकरी करनी चाहिए मेरी क्वालिफिकेशन एमएससी थी।2-3 विज्ञापन देखकर इंटरव्यू भी देने गई पर बात बनी नहीं ,फिर मैंने सोचा कि बस अब और इंटरव्यू नहीं दूंगी। कुछ दिनों बाद मेरी एक सहेली लखनऊ से शाम को मेरे घर आई और लखनऊ रेलवे स्टेशन के एक पीर बाबा की उदी उसने मुझे दी मैंने उसे ग्रहण किया ,अगले ही दिन *दोपहर करीब 12:30 बजे मेरी कॉलोनी की एक और सहेली जो कि एक स्कूल में टीचर भी हैं आकर मुझसे ऊपर वाले घर की पड़ोसन के बारे में पूछने लगी कि वह कहां गई है उसके घर पर ताला लगा है तब मुझे पता नहीं था तो मैंने कहा कि मुझे तो नहीं मालूम कि वह कहां है। तो उसने मुझसे पूछा कि क्या वह मेरे ही घर पर बैठ कर इंतजार कर ले।और वह मेरे घर पर बैठकर उसका इंतजार करने लगी इसी बीच उसने मुझे बताया कि वह जिस स्कूल में काम करती

है वहां पर एक अर्जेंट टीचर की वैकेंसी है जिसके लिए वह उस पड़ोसन को अपने साथ स्कूल ले जाना चाहती है क्योंकि उसके पास b.ed की डिग्री थी. पर काफी देर इंतजार करने के बाद भी वह नहीं आई तो मेरी फ्रेंड ने मुझसे कहा कि तुम चलो मेरे साथ मेरे स्कूल में। मैं एकदम से हैरान रह गई क्योंकि सुबह से काम में लगी थी अभी तक स्नान पूजा कुछ भी नहीं किया था और फिर मेरे पास b.ed की डिग्री भी नहीं थी मेरी फ्रेंड ने मुझसे कहा कि तुम चलो इंटरव्यू दे दो अगर बात समझ में आए तो ठीक है उनको ठीक लगा तो लोग रखेंगे नहीं तो तुम को समझ में ना आए तो तुम भी मना कर सकती हो. उसने मुझे कहा चलने में हर्ज ही क्या है।फिर उसने मुझे अपने साथ ओरिजिनल मार्कशीट और सर्टिफिकेट लेने के लिए कहा जिसे ढूंढने में आधा घंटा और लग गया इसके बाद हम दोनों स्कूल गए उसने मुझे अपनी प्रिंसिपल से मिलवाया और फिर वह चली गई ।प्रिंसिपल ने मेरा इंटरव्यू लिया और लेकर कहा कि आप डेमो (presentation)दे दो ,मैंने उसे साफ-साफ बताया कि मैंने कभी टीचर की नौकरी नहीं की और ना ही मेरे पास डिग्री है b.ed की। मुझे डेमो देने में हिचकिचाहट हो रही थी तो उसने मुझे एक किताब देकर कहा कल तैयारी कर के आना और डेमो दे देना ।मैं घर वापस आ गई और अपनी किसी एक और फ्रेंड की मदद से डेमो की तैयारी की और अगले दिन जाकर स्कूल में डेमो दिया , अभी डेमो पूरा खत्म भी नहीं हुआ था कि बीच में ही उठ कर उसने मुझे कहा कि तुम अभी से टीचर की नौकरी ज्वाइन करो. मुझे तो विश्वास ही नहीं हुआ इतना बड़ा स्कूल जो बिना b.ed के किसी टीचर को नहीं रखता है उसने मुझे नौकरी ज्वाइन करने को कहा , और वह नौकरी जिसके लिए मैंने कोई आवेदन नहीं किया था मैं तो घर पर बैठी हुई थी बाबा ने घर तक मेरी नौकरी पहुंच वाई इससे ज्यादा मैं और क्या कहूं,साईं बाबा मन की बात जानते हैं उन्हें पता है भक्तों की इच्छा के बारे में,मेरी खुशी का तो ठिकाना ही नहीं था और यह सब सिर्फ और सिर्फ साईं बाबा की वजह से हुआ. जिनकी वजह से 42 वर्ष की आयु में मैंने अपने जीवन में नौकरी की शुरुआत की। और यही नहीं बाबा की कृपा और आशीर्वाद से 45 वर्ष की आयु में मैंने अपना b.ed भी संपूर्ण किया। और एक बात बताना चाहूंगी कि जॉइनिंग के बाद जब मैं पहली बार स्कूल गई तो मुझे प्रिंसिपल ने कहा कि लाइब्रेरी से जाकर अपनी क्लासेस की जो बुक हैंउन्हें ईशु करवा लो ,जब मैं लाइब्रेरी में गई तो किसी कक्षा के छात्र वहां बैठे पढ़ाई कर रहे थे और जिस किताब पर मेरी नजर सबसे पहले गईवह किताब साईं बाबा की एक कॉमिक थी जिस के कवर पेज पर साईं बाबा की बहुत खूबसूरत सी तस्वीर बनी हुई थी ।क्या यह भी एक संयोग था?बाबा जानते हैं अपने भक्तों की मन की बात और उसे पूरा करने के लिए बाबा

हर संभव प्रयास करके उसे पूरा करते हैं ।उन्होंने उदी के रूप में मुझे आशीर्वाद देकर मुझे सफल बनाया ।बाबा अपने भक्तों की हर छोटी -बड़ी इच्छा का ध्यान रखते हैं, और स्नेह एवं श्रद्धा से उसे पूरा करते हैं। हमें भी बाबा श्रद्धा और सबुरी रखने को कहते हैं। अपने सभी भक्तों को बाबा बहुत बहुत प्यार करते हैं।
*साईं बाबा की कृपा और इच्छा से ही मैं यह लेख लिख पाई ।उनकी कृपा के बिना इस कार्य का पूर्ण होना संभव नहीं था।बाबा मैं आपकी कृतज्ञ और ऋणी हूं ।
      ?शुकराना बाबा शुकराना?*
?जय साईं राम जय साईं देवा?
?श्री सच्चिदानंद सद्गुरु *साईंनाथ महाराज की जय?*
?ओम साईं राम?

14
Bineesh Balakrishnan

Dr. Bineesh Balakrishnan is a practising Physiatrist (PMR specialist) & published author. His first book 'Freigeist... An unfettered soul' was released in March 2018...He is an ardent devotee of Sai Bhagawan...

Humble Pranams

Every morning, You bathe me in sunbeams,
I am grateful for being Your humble devotee.
Come rain or shine, You'll always be by my side.
You're my father, mother, brother, & friend, dear Sai!

Your love for me keeps me going on,
And gives me shelter from all storms.
The lessons I learned at Your lotus feet,
Make me feel at peace, and complete.

The solace I find, as I look into Your stolid eyes,
Helps me heal all the pain that I have inside.
Your eleven divine promises mean more to me,
Than all the treasures in all the known galaxies.

My life only started to make sense,
When You cradled me in Your hands.
Please do pardon all my mistakes,
And protect me from greed & hate.

Help me to heal hurt souls & aching hearts,
To be a beacon of love and hope in the dark.
I want to spread Your love, wisdom and glory,
So that it will help heal the whole of humanity.

15
Dinakar Reddy

Dinakar Reddy finds peace in writing stories and poetry while juggling between shift works. He hails from a small town in Kadapa district of Andhra Pradesh.

फोंडनेस फॉर डाईती

Shirdiwale Saibaba

Lust made me behave like a puppet,
Anger is burning my self-consciousness,
Greed is searching for ways to fill me with negativity,
Emotional Attachments are causing suffocation to my soul,
Ego pushes me towards making bad decisions,
Jealousy is acting to ruin my happiness,
When the arishadvargas are tormenting me,
I ran into you,
And I found light while praying you,
Your teachings made me relieve from negative thoughts,
Shraddha and Saburi wrote on the wall behind your statue,
Makes me feel hopeful when I am in distress,
Let my devotion detaches me from arishdvargas,
Let me serve you with the Nava vidha Bhakti,
Let me sing your glories,
Let me worship you every day,
Hey Shirdiwale Sai Baba,
Let me chant your name with the belief in my heart,
As you said,
You will listen and come to bless me

16
Pawan Dubey

Pawan Dubey is a writer, who love to write Hindi, Urdu, English poetries and Stories as well. Where he uses his writing passion for social activities to write social awareness content. He also does Open Mic to spread positive vibes, love and motivation by his voice. . Pawan Dubey is a co-author of two anthology books named as "Shabd Sangini" and "Imagination". Talking about his honours, He honoured from Dr. Nusrat Mehadi (Secretary, Urdu academy. Department of culture) and Ms Krishna Gour(MLA, Bhopal) for his writing. He was also selected for Perl Event BITS PILANI Hyderabad in top 5 writers among Bhopal city

"साई है"

भक्त की प्रीत, भक्ति का गीत साई है।
आँखों की तृप्ति, जीवन का संगीत साई है।।

संध्या-प्रातः वंदन, ईश दर्शन साई है।
आत्मरूप, शक्ति स्वरूप, जीवन के मीत साई है।।

इच्छा की अनुभूति, इच्छापूर्ति साई है।
हार में भी संतुष्टि, जीवन की जीत साई है।।

मन के विचार, मन-विकार संहारक साई है।
हृदय के भाव, जीवन के पुनीत साई है।।

साई रचित, सुगम दृश्य सचित साई है।
सृष्टि हित, सहज प्रतीत, जीवन की रीत साई है।।

प्रीत- प्रेम, प्रिय
तृप्ति- आनंद, संतुष्टि
मीत- मित्र
पुनीत- पवित्र
सचित- ज्ञान युक्त
रीत- रीति

17
"भक्ति की नींद"

भक्ति की नींद में ही मुझको रहना है,
बाबा, स्वप्न दर्शन हो आपका बार बार..
अखियों का मेरी, यही कहना है..

जागने पर यह जग रास नही आता,
कई ख़याल और ख़यालात का,
मंज़र ही बार बार नज़र आता..

साई दर्श से, हृदय प्रफुल्लित होता मेरा..
साई कृपा से आनन्दित, यह जीवन मेरा..

साई-भक्ति का रस पीना है,
भक्ति की नींद में ही..
बाबा मुझको रहना है,

18
"मुझमें साई..तुझमें साई.."

साई श्रद्धा का सागर,
साई सबुरी की गागर..

साई शक्ति की विभूति,
साई भक्ति अनुभूति..

साई ज्योति की आस,
साई ही अटूट विश्वास..

साई से सब, साई से ही अब..

मुझमें साई.. तुझमें साई..
मेरे साई.. बाबा साई..

www.ingramcontent.com/pod-product-compliance
Lightning Source LLC
LaVergne TN
LVHW021738060526
838200LV00052B/3340